The Porous Desert
David Chorlton

with cover design and art work by the author

FUTURECYCLE PRESS
Mineral Bluff, Georgia

SECOND EDITION
Copyright © 2007, 2012 David Chorlton
All Rights Reserved

Published by FutureCycle Press
Mineral Bluff, Georgia, USA

ISBN 978-1-938853-14-2

Contents

The Porous Desert 5
The Night Fox 6
Living with Drought 8
Seeking Directions 10
Dry 11
Verde Canyon 12
Spring Birding 14
Writing in the Desert 16
Desert Nocturne 17
A Desert Primer 18
Listening to Stars 19
Desert Character 20
Notes from the White Mountains 21
Map 22
Ponderosa 23
Condor 24
Somewhere Near Calexico 25
Highway Religion 26
Emptiness 27
Monsoon 28
Summer Calendar 29
Reprise 30
December 31
Christmas Bird Count in the Desert 32
Winter Drought 33
Proofreading 34
February 6th 35
February 7th 36
February 8th 37
February 9th 38
Glass of Water 39

The Gods	40
February 21st	41
February 22nd	42
February 23rd	43
February 25th	44
Sky Watch	45
Tracking the Gray Hawk	46
March 6th	47
Spring	48
Madera Canyon, Midnight and Midday	49
White Mountain Hours	50
Encounters	52
Living with Doves	53
Interstate Sky	54
Three Lies About Moths	55
Riparian Darkness	56
Illusions	57
The Lost Dutchman	58
Acknowledgements	59

Illustrations: Saguaro, p. 7; Verde Canyon, p. 13; Vermillion Flycatcher, p. 23; Saguaro, p. 43; Gray Hawk, p. 47; Madera Canyon, p. 48; The Lost Dutchman, p. 57

The Porous Desert

The desert's bones run crooked
beneath its skin, packed
in layers of thirst
that crack with pressure from the core
pushing them back
into the light

where scorpions crawl like beads of sweat
across rocks
with their stockpile of illusions:

ore whispering from the earth
for somebody to find it,
the wet reflection
of dry sand,
a calcium deity rising from behind a peak
to survey
its last chance to be alone.

The rain is scented creosote
here; it gathers in a flash
and briefly soaks
the ribs and femurs that remain
from the parting of muscle and sinew

before dripping through
the diaphragm of the earth
to mark the passing centuries,
each one draining
faster than the last.

The Night Fox

At midnight in a time of drought
the lamps around the house make thirsty light
and insects drawn toward them
settle in their heat

each one swollen with a drop
of glowing water.
A hundred days have risen
and gone back to the sun
in a swarm of bees.
On the hundred and first

a bird limps down from the sky
and pecks an empty bowl
until we fill it.
On the hundred and second
some clouds appear to tease us.
Day one hundred and three

slips into its night
like an arm into a sleeve
holding in the warmth.
The day after
we sharpen the sunlight
on a whetstone
and the one after that

drips through the waist
of the hourglass.
No more measuring

the time since rain.
A dusty wind
has blown itself away
leaving the scent
of desert in the city.
We go out into the blue
of the early hours
and look

for the fox
who knows where the last
water bubbles
from a hidden spring.

Living with Drought

We know we are living with drought
when rain becomes so precious
we wear the drops on a chain
around our necks.

Touching the ground each morning
to feel for dew
reveals our insecurity.
We beg the passing clouds
to stop, invoke gods

known to be extinct
for a miracle, and polish
our faucets for luck.
Wildflower season finds us

counting roadside blooms
for reassurance. Vacationing
in ghost towns
we make friends with fate,
but too late. The owls

are already staring at us
accusingly, the lizards
have us in their sights,
and bats pour into the sky

without waiting for dark.
We try sleep
as a final refuge,

only to wake
after an hour, reaching
for the glass at our bedside
and seeing by the light
of the scorpion inside it.

Seeking Directions

In a landscape of secrets, only the survivors
of a previous visit know
where to look. They alone

see the ridges of light pierced with thorns
as they rise
from shallow roots, the folds
in rock where the sun
cannot reach, and the names
of every shrub and cactus
pushing through
like a hoarse voice
the silent surface of the desert.

They have the map
printed on their skin
of the path toward the hidden stream
where at nightfall
the animals come

for their ration of water and darkness.
This is their country,

for which no passport has been issued,
for which there is no guide book,
where the compass needle plays its wayward tricks

and true north exists
wherever you decide.

Dry

Dry is the shade of light on a mountain
jutting suddenly from a flat
expanse of desert
and the ribs in a dead saguaro
are dry as they bend toward the ground
which is so dry it glows.
A cholla stripped of its thorns
is fibre and holes reaching into the dry air
like the hand of a man
who lost his way
and fell through his shadow.
The hooks on a barrel cactus are dry
as are the spears on the yucca
and the stars growing from the flesh of the senita.
The forecast is for dry
and when the centipede crawls from the crevice
in a rock, its orange segments
appear as drops of water
walking on a hundred legs.

Verde Canyon

I
Those who make the journey
back toward a landscape's origins

travel slowly, a year at a time,
until they disappear

into the space
where a lake once filled the basin.

II
The red walls of the canyon
are home to swallows
and the eagle

whose shadow ripples
like a scarf

fallen from the sky.

III
Sunlight washes over water
as a heron
watches for the silver
trembling of a fish

and a train passes on the bank
returning from mines beneath the glowing rocks

where darkness yields its ore.

IV
Someone calls
into the canyon

and the voice tears apart
on an ocotillo's thorns.

Spring Birding

I
As cactus wrens fluff
out their feathers
a low-pitched rasping
is the voice
of the mercury rising
in the year's thermometer.

II
We scan the saguaro
with glasses raised and focused
on the spot where a Gila woodpecker
appears against the drop of darkness
drilled into the ribs. We watch it
come and go with the red streak burning
on its crown, with light
strumming the black and white stripes
along its back.

III
A rustle in the leafy undergrowth
of riparian land
turns brown as two Abert's towhees
rummage with their tails raised
in a visual rhyme.

IV
A western tanager
in the paloverde is pausing on its journey
to higher elevation, a brief chorus
of colour splashing
before the desert stills
beneath summer's weight.

V
Over a city
that is bigger each spring than it was at the last
a great blue heron
moves like the memory of water
with a brushstroke of late sun
gilding the edge of its wing.

Writing in the Desert

Once you have entered the desert
a lock behind you clicks. A new vocabulary
floods your tongue and leaves you struggling
to pronounce the words. After the first year
you learn that silence is the official language
here. The longer you stay
the shorter the book you came to write becomes
until the manuscript fits on the wings
of a moth. Each dusk, a lifetime's work
draws closer to the flame.

Desert Nocturne

Owls move silently as wishes through the dark,
their yellow eyes burning with concentration
from the soft and mottled textures
of their faces. When stars appear above a mountain
in the desert the heat of the day
releases its grip on our throats
and we who have chosen this landscape
for its mystery inhale moonlight. It washes
through our lungs and we watch the shadows
fly away to roost after we exhale them.

A Desert Primer

In the skeletal remains of cholla
you feel heat
as solid form, with fibres
twisted into the shape of thirst
and in the saguaro
you find light
that stands up straight
with thorns that snag the shadows
as they pass. The eyes of a coyote
will turn to water
as you look into them.
Ocotillo reach out of the earth
with a blossom held at the tip
of each strand, the colour of a hundred
degrees still rising. Walk
in the path of last year's rain
through an arroyo. Look away
at the horizon stretched
as wide as you have ever seen it,
taut enough to snap
beneath the impact of your gaze.

Listening to Stars

We travel along a saguaro-lined road
to see Jupiter's moons. Mountains
approach us, glowing with late
afternoon light, and drop back
toward the horizons
leaving us a clear run to the clearing

where we arrive as nighthawks
first soar from the grass
and cut the breaking
darkness into ribbons.
The stars appear
between their speeding wings.
A comet

drags its frosty tail
from behind a cloud.
The desert sinks into a bed of sounds;
insects tuning their voices,
a cough from the dry
earth. We turn a lens

until the rings encircling Saturn
are in focus, until the undergrowth rustles
with the white noise of the universe.

Desert Character

The farther behind I leave the past, the closer I am to forging my own character.

Isabelle Eberhardt

Every spring a sphinx moth
fixes itself to the screen door, a message
from the present
to tell me another page of history
has been overwritten.
The white winged doves arrive

from their other homes, and lizards
crawl out from between the bricks
with the story of winter sleep
in code on their backs.
As the temperature rises

the black bees find their way back
to their hole in the bougainvillea vine
and geckos appear at night
clinging to the doorframe
with stars at the tips of their limbs.
To listen to the towhees rustle on the ground

I go outside
where the light has a serrated edge
and the desert sparkles
in the waist of an hourglass.

Notes from the White Mountains

I   *South Fork*
From lava rock, thistle, and wind
a road winds down
to a stream where time and lightning
have marked the pines. Insects
as transparent as the water
hang on shafts of light. A Weidemeyer's Admiral
opens and closes its wings, a warbler's face
appears red against green,
and aspen leaves flow through a whisper.

II   *Big Lake*
A cloudbank rolls
from the dividing line
of earth and sky
dark with rain, to frame the kestrel
with rapidly beating wings
in suspended flight
pinning its body
to the stillness preceding a storm.

III   *Mexican Hay Lake*
The summer long calls
of a tanager
sound in the pines
surrounding a lake gone dry:
drought's footprint.

IV   *Thompson Trail*
In the tallest firs
sound has a shadow.
The kinglet's trill
precedes each peal of thunder.

Map

The map shows trails and altitude.
It indicates the rivers and the roads
that wind between them.
Forests are the patches printed darker
than the hills. We use it
as a guide when we hike. We take a yellow marker
to remember for the next time.
Two years pass. Our map
is the same, but we can't find the trail.
The forest doesn't reach
the lake anymore. We count fewer larks
than the last time. Another year.
The map is folded smaller.
A lark sings from a fence post.
We walk in a circle around it,
fold the map again
until it is the size of a postage stamp,
until it fits on the envelope
addressed to a senator, with an appeal
to leave us this much of the land
by which to remember the rest.

Ponderosa

— the will of a tree; something that frightens you.
                                        D. H. Lawrence

In a density of pines
the mind has a shadow.
It wraps us

in a ring of darkness
and reveals the will
holding trees to the earth.
We stroke their bark

to feel the weather beneath;
calendars of rain
and drought.
We come to them to be still,

to find patience
and to listen
for a breath of wind

or birdsong. We don't move,
even when the cutting
begins. One by one
we disappear

leaving only our shoes
to record where we stood.

Condor

The condor stares down into time;
the work of years
with a knife edge, of seasons
that sand away and polish
surfaces then grind them into wizened planes
stacked one above another
until the cliffs hang on a talon.
The daily passage of shadows

from rim to canyon rim
and the final drop
of light disappearing from the highest rock
are nothing but sighs
to a bird suspended from the sun

while the minutes drip
from its wings, evaporating
before they can reach the river

moving at the pace of history,
water burning deep
into pages of stone.

Somewhere Near Calexico

What is it like, we ask the sunlight,
to live in the place we are passing
surrounded by silence and dust
where the land is nailed down at its edges
by a thirsty fence? Who would choose
to wake up every day and see the heat
refuse to give up
its birthright? What is there to do
besides sitting back and gazing
at the minutes chasing the hours
through sagebrush? There is nobody for miles
to wash for, just a radio signal
coaxing a foreign language
out of the receiver to sparkle
a moment in the listener's ear
before sleep; the wind
in translation.

Highway Religion

The desert keeps its good looks
for a while west of Phoenix
then it turns honest.
The hours evaporate

along the highway
between truck stops in which
the temperature never changes,
where you can buy a souvenir
made in China, a book
about the afterlife,

and a cassette tape for the road
that talks when you are lonely
about Jesus' coming. Perhaps
he will appear between

the dry mesquite,
thumbing a ride to salvation.
Perhaps he will speak Spanish,
and carry no passport.
Or perhaps it's just a story

that made its way back to this desert
where illusions
are the standard currency,
a promised land
with the next promise
seventy miles away.

Emptiness

From one kind of void to another
we travel first
past the abandoned
grandstand west of Phoenix
where a dust devil twines
around fingers of light
crossed for luck
in the ghost race of winds through the creosote,

stopping at a desert
convenience store
splendid in its isolation,
a throwaway palace,

past trailer park driveways
of manicured gravel,

sandward to the dunes
lying naked,

and between a bombing range and a proving ground
beside ankle high vegetation
on the highway toward a sign
indicating emptiness
in which to park in the heat

with *No Facilities*
Handicapped Friendly

Monsoon

The monsoon arrives without warning,
knocks down the door, walks in
and disengages the evaporate cooler
with a sweep of its arm
before asking for a drink with a glacier
in the cup. It can't stop hugging us
with its brawny arms, breathing
its steam train breath
and sitting down in a pool of sweat
to talk. *Do you enjoy living in the desert?*
it says. *I do. I like it when the crackling in the dunes
is the sound of light
soaking into sand, when the drip
inside a mountain is a memory
nobody claims, when a whisper passes
through the creosote
and the sky spits lightning through its broken teeth.*
And like the uninvited guest it is
it settles in, too heavy to remove,
acting like a friend we lost last year,
offended that we never called. We do our best
to live with it, thankful for the scent
of rain in its armpits and the thunder in its voice
while we wait for the sound of its footsteps
as it goes away, the soggy plod
we are thankful for when the ground is moist again.

Summer Calendar

Each page on summer's calendar
is a thirsty tongue
turning over, keeping time
between the blooming of the ocotillo
and the storm clouds
gathering with a promise
of rain. They cast

no shadows; the sun
burns through them
daily, digging its claws
into rocks and pecking at the spaces
between ironwood trees. As one day

gives way to another
a leaf of darkness slips
between them,
thin as a moth's wing.
Before sleep

we pull it over us
and take refuge in
the night's velvet breath.

Reprise

At summer's end a vulture rises on a thermal
and turns toward another country.
A river stumbles on its path
between cottonwoods, and in a blink
of our eyes the vermilion flycatchers
disappear. We look over our shoulders

at threads of water on the meadow
where a storm cloud hung while we sought shelter
beneath an aching pine. Desert mountains
are lodged in the corners of our eyes,
a thrush's song keeps playing on rewind
while we retrace our route

from the blooming ocotillo
to the woodpecker's tapping on bark
and watch the doves fly south
past a flash of dry lightning.

December

An empty nest floats through winter
in the fingers of a tree
scratched against a mountain
at rest.

The snow on the upper reaches
glows from the light in the rock
packed beneath it.

Grasses whose lives have paused
rustle at the passing
of the coyote who never sleeps.
And on the last breath of sun

a chill flows out of the forest
sharpening its teeth
on tree bark and stones.

Christmas Bird Count in the Desert

We're out in the desert invisible
to tourists, who prefer to visit photographs
in travel magazines. The mesquite
here is thin on the ground
and the ground is so dry this winter
we can hear the bark
on a tree stump crack while we listen
for the calls of white-crowned sparrows.
From Rainbow Wash
we hike to the cattle tank, glasses raised
all the way, then stoop to negotiate
the thorns and fallen branches
around a pool of water
that opens like an eye to watch
the fighter planes overhead
as they tear holes in the peace. After checking off
verdins and gnatcatchers
we reflect on the state of nature
in a thirsty world. Through pencil cholla
whose needles assault us
we carry the image of bones
stripped bare by the sun
and study the melted ribs
of a collapsed saguaro, raise our glasses
to a loggerhead shrike,
and toast its presence with our eyes,
relieved to find survival
in a landscape marked for roads
where the map is obsolete
as soon as it is drawn.

Winter Drought

We're living in a rich man's winter
with sun enough for a January tan
and the desert around us
in its finery of browns and yellow
too dry to glow. The last rain
came ninety days ago, washing summer
away at the tip of a lightning flash.
We look to the sky for a sign,
finding only a reflection of the ground
on which we stand. Cactus needles
sew arroyos into the clouds,
a riverbed stretches from horizon
to horizon, and the light hangs torn
on the wings of a circling hawk.
Some days we follow the highway
just to see where it goes; it feels like
racing on a tightrope strung across a canyon
millions of years in the making
with no space to turn back.

Proofreading

This is the detail work
of flossing between the letters.
After a hundred days without rain
it feels like looking at an unblemished sky
in the hope of a cloud. Twenty pages
set correctly. Another dry night,
and a sunrise so clear
it spells out a spring with no wildflowers.
After forty pages not even
a missing period. I look outside
to clear my eyes. Bright sun.
A cough in the atmosphere. The light
between lines of print
is dazzling me. My mouth is dry.
I can taste a summer of fires
as I pause before reading
the final page, and scribble
with my red pen in the margin
just to test the flow of ink
and leave a mark to show
that someone was here, and that reading
this page felt like
raking dry leaves from the sky.

February 6th

The desert turns in its winter sleep,
waiting for fingers of rain to probe the deep places
where seeds lie dormant. The television station
broadcast last Monday's news show this morning,
suggesting that time flows in all directions
and nothing happens differently
no matter how intently we watch. We set the alarm
to wake us when a shower breaks
but another day floats between the clouds
as we turn back the pages of a calendar so dry
they crack at a touch.

February 7th

Lawn sprinklers perpetuate the illusion
of normality in a season
out of tune with an Earth
from which everyone is trying to secure
their portion with a down payment
of stolen water. Explorers around the globe

have discovered a new jungle
where our imaginations swing
on hanging vines and we're sweating
from the thought of humidity

on another day of sand
running through our fingers.

February 8th

The forest has begun talking back
at the drought, one hundred and thirteen days
after the last taste
of water landed fresh
from a cloud that left its shadow
torn among the boughs
of a pine tree
where the first flame took hold
and lit up the air
for others to follow.

February 9th

We're logging on to tomorrow, divining
our way through the hours
as they drip from a rusty faucet.
We type in the address: www.water.com

but it comes up dry, so we try a search
for rain. The first result
is a tease: *On February 6, 1896, 3.86*
inches of rain fell in Philadelphia,
setting a maximum daily record. Tonight

there will be a meeting to discuss
the heat island in our urban region
which spreads further and digs
deeper by the day, down to the ruins
of a past civilization: clay pots

still bearing the potter's fingerprints,
and the tracks her sandals
left behind when she looked into the future,
saw us, and walked the other way.

Glass of Water

Fill a glass with water. Place it
by the window so the light
can soak inside it. Stare hard
until you feel thirst
take root in your throat. Relish
the thought of touching the rim
to your lips, and the moment
moisture first runs
into your mouth. Think of a coyote
slipping through the dark
to sip from a pool
in a hollow of rock. Think
of the same rock
after a season with no rain.
When you tip the glass
you discover the water was just
an illusion. Think of the sky
polished smooth as porcelain.
Think of a storm in a teacup.

The Gods

The grackles are drinking mirrors
while coyotes sand the bed
of what used to be a pond
with their tongues
and the hallucinations
that rise from the asphalt
when we drive to find an oasis
are dancing to the tune
the sky plays. The weather channel
broadcasts reruns
from last year's storms
to keep morale alive, and the spines
on our books are cracking
in dry air. Nobody remembers
how the rain dance goes.
The gods don't answer
when we call, but bet in higher increments
every day as they roll their dice
on the roof of the world.

February 21st

The mockingbirds seem not to know
it hasn't rained since October
from the way they bounce
in mating dances
and the mourning doves could be forgiven
for believing water comes
out of the earth
considering the sprinklers fanning
moisture over lawns. The sparrows
perched at the edge of the bowls
we set out in the yard
dip their beaks into the water
as if plastic were a well
with no bottom. The sun comes up,
casts another round of dry shadows
and falls behind the telegraph lines
where starlings hang like black raindrops.

February 22nd

The seven day forecast has been recycled
for another term. Smoke on the horizon
tells us there is more
of the same to come. The crystal ball
is filled with ashes, shoots peer
from the flower beds
unsure of whether to emerge,
and the trees
reach out with their boughs
to feel for moisture in the air,
while the newscast tells us to stay inside
because there is nothing to wash
away the pollution. But the sunsets
are so beautiful when the rays
illuminate dust, we can't resist
the view of red where a single cloud
blossoms behind the palm fronds.

February 23rd

It's been so long without precipitation
we're beginning to hallucinate
and plant illusory grass
beneath our postcard sky
then coax it with recordings
of rainforest storms
that we play each afternoon
to plant the tropics in our ears
while the desert drains through an hourglass
and leaves us nothing but the light
to remember it by.

February 25th

The sound of wind chimes on a clear day
and the quietly hissing sprinklers
mark the calendar with air and water
as we place another dry cross
to record our longing for a storm
that will rinse the edges of the trees
back to green. Without magic
to offer, we're helpless
and thirsty for dark skies,
listening to the slow wind's music
for the long absent rumble
in a minor key to burst the sky open.

Sky Watch

Some days a patch of sky
turns into a falcon
and perches in the tall pine
at Holly and 3rd Avenue.

On other days the blue
arcs over us
without a break
in memory's driest winter.
Sometimes when I'm looking

in the hope of rain
I see a kestrel come to rest
as stillness on a fuse
until it spears a flock of starlings.
Today the clouds provided

a backdrop for the gray hawk
farther north than ever before.
It stayed above me

long enough to display
the streaks on its breast
and the dark tips of its primaries.
Its presence speaks in favour

of illusion, of a long
awaited storm
moving past us on the wing.

Tracking the Gray Hawk

The first sighting was a ghost
bird in a dead tree
on a day as pale
as the bird's name. The second

was more sound
than sight, detonating into
wingflap from the dark
interior of foliage.
Next were the circles

it drew on the light
with a few slow beats
and a glide, while its status

veered from impossible
to accidental, not unlike
that of the people who plant grass
as an investment

and abduct a river
to keep it moist. Then the bird came
closer than doubt,

hung on a thread, spread itself wide,
and printed its image
on a cloud.

March 6th

Rain watch continues while the water boils
for tea, while the shower head
sprays faithfully, while the garden hose
discharges a few gallons more
on the flowerbed, and while we reconstitute
the food we buy in packets. Every twist
of the faucet brings a miracle
masquerading as a birthright, and another day
hangs on the line with the rags
that were used to wash the floor
upon which our reflections
float as they would on a lake polished smooth
by an unforgiving sun.

Spring

After the voices of sparrows have changed
into those of doves
that fly north in March, after
the end of one drought
becomes the start of another, after
the splash of wildflowers,
the moths appear with moonlight
dusted onto their wings
as they emerge from between the pages
of winter's unread books.

Madera Canyon, Midnight and Midday

I
Streaming between the sycamore
and oak, one bat
follows another, almost touching
my face while I listen
to an owl in the ash tree
answer the whip-poor-will in the grass,
and watch a skunk
scent the moonlight with spray
as the startled hairs
along its tail stand up.

II
Sunlight burns the edges of shadows
cast by mesquite. The ground
is still too dry for breeding
and the forecast is for hawks
while sparrows wait
for clouds to form. We memorise
their calls from a recording,
note plumage details from our guide,
and see Box Canyon Road
paved with silence
leading straight ahead to where
the Santa Ritas
are branded into the sky.

White Mountain Hours

Waking in half light
when green is still blue
and no shadows appear
we follow the elk
in procession along
the grass slope
with the thread of a gaze
weaving through them.
On a pond that floats
in a high meadow
the beaver leaves a ripple
where he parts the water
with his nose
as the first hawk glides
out of the sun
tipping to the pull
of each wing in its turn
with clouds already forming
on his back. They break
apart in patches
on the wide and treeless
space the horned larks
occupy, and on the bed
of the dry lake where
a pronghorn grazes alone.

☼

The trail obeys the West Fork
of the river, and draws
thunder at noon
when a falcon shakes
lightning from its wing

into old growth silence.
Sky calls and responds
to the hermit thrushes
in their nests
of fluted song.

☼

After the draining of light
from wild iris
as a prelude to the final
swallow flight
the wooded slopes edge higher
into night
and the calls of silver throated wolves.

Encounters

The animals that walk into our lives
take their chances
and with luck they walk away.
A black tom

who won't let us touch him
sits by the door each morning
waiting for food
then he melts down the wall
and disappears. The bear

we met once on a trail
wasn't interested in us, and looked
for a moment before
ambling away into the green shadows

of higher ground. Whether habit
or surprise, these presences
are pinned

like medals for solidarity
with the wild
to our lapels. But the lion
doesn't know, when drought drives him
out of his range,

that human fear has the power
of thirst

and the untamed scent
of gunshot
hangs a moment before
it too drifts away.

Living with Doves

I took the first one in
because its kind would not survive
in the wild, then felt sorry
for its loneliness
and sought a mate accustomed
to captivity. One egg
hatched. Another dove landed
on my neighbour's wall
without trying to escape.
The four of them are free
to fly around the room I work in
and to perch above
the computer screen
while I access my imagination,
wondering what it is like
to be an animal or bird
in a human world. Rivers soak
into the earth, forests
thin, and machines grind the desert
into submission. All the while
I juggle words
into another appeal
against the loss of species
but on some days
the alphabet falls apart.
Living without language
is a start. Once I have mastered
the sounds of the doves
I will learn other voices
of the wild, walk through the city
and let out a cry
to ask why we are so few here,
we wolves.

Interstate Sky

Orange clouds are darkening into blue
electrified by a sunset
that gilds the freight cars on a train
whose long, slow, grumbling horn
cries to the full moon
from the chambers of its oily, iron heart.

Three Lies About Moths

As the hawk to the tall eucalyptus
a chill returns to the night
and moths for a day
find shade in the leaves
of bougainvillea and orange trees
before their journeys through the stars.

☼

In previous lives
moths were books that stood unread
on library shelves. When the lights went out
they eased themselves free of confinement
and nobody knew in the morning
what mysterious force
opened exactly the pages
whose text described the moon.

☼

A moth remembers
the world before technology
made it spin at the pace
of greed. A creature
close to dust, it drank
one raindrop for a lifetime
and knew it was enough.

Riparian Darkness

A desert river winds
around edges of rock
when the moon has risen
and pulls the water
with its dusty light.
Flowing faster at night

it sings with the voices
of stones that have aged
in silence on the bed
until their time
came to soften into sound.
The wingbeats of owls

and the pale padded steps
of coyotes
are its guide as it runs
blind through the heart
of midnight with a jaguar's
strength and the innocent

blink of its prey
before it disappears.

Illusions

On the street next to yours, you think you see
a fox with its tail brushing up
against the darkness, then the pale

owl like a whisper
sweeps past your ear, and the segments

of a mantis assemble
themselves right
before your eyes. Even by day, you blink

at the sight of a bird nesting
in a thimble while another

spreads its wings as wide
as wonder on the sky
and on the ground the sunlight
flows from the tail of a snakeskin

to the head
where it drips as venom
onto dry, dry earth.

The Lost Dutchman

In the park of lost mines
the trails run in circles and lead
back to humble beginnings
after a climb to the view
through brittlebush, Mormon tea, and mistletoe
of mountains pressing back
against clouds that deliver
rain as rare as precious metals
at summer's end. This is where
prospectors took their coffee pots
and bad teeth with beans
for every meal in search of the vein
that would open up and shine
through the darkness in a shaft
running deep in their imaginations
while winds slipped between
the arms of old saguaro.
The closest they came to gold
was light clinging to the needles
on jumping cholla that snagged
their weary clothes
when they grew tired of rock
ringing against their shovels
and their faces had more creases
than their maps. It was
of little consolation to them
that rock wrens sang, mesquite hummed
in the heat, or hawks descended
from clear skies when they rolled
up their shadows to leave
and coughed up a last
globe of phlegm
that was dry before it reached the ground.

Acknowledgements

Abbey: A Desert Primer, March 6th
Apocalypse: The Porous Desert
Avocet: The Porous Desert, Spring Birding, December, Living with Doves, Tracking the Gray Hawk
Bogg: Dry, Highway Religion
Bosco: Reprise, February 25th
Brevities: Interstate Sky
California Quarterly: Sky Watch
Canyon Echo: Ponderosa, Notes from the White Mountains, Winter Drought
Connecticut Review: Verde Canyon
Desert Voices: Glass of Water
Edgz: Postcards from the Border, Christmas Bird Count, The Lost Dutchman
Free Verse: Madera Canyon, Midnight and Midday
The Higginsville Reader: The Night Fox
Kimera: December
Lilliput Review: February 23rd, Spring
Main Street Rag: The Gods
Merge: Desert Nocturne, Proofreading
Parting Gifts: Writing in the Desert, Christmas Bird Count in the Desert
Poetry at Lehani's: Three Lies About Moths
Poetry Depth Quarterly: Seeking Directions, Listening to Stars, February 6th, February 7th, February 8th, February 9th
Poetry Super Highway: February 21st, February 22nd, February 23rd
Skidrow Penthouse: Summer Calendar
Slipstream: Highway Religion
Thrift: Monsoon
Thunder Sandwich: Living with Drought, Emptiness
Voices on the Wind: Condor, Somewhere Near Calexico, Encounter
The Wandering Hermit Review: Desert Character
Zillah: Map

About FutureCycle Press

FutureCycle Press is dedicated to publishing lasting English-language poetry and flash fiction books, chapbooks, and anthologies in both print-on-demand and ebook formats. Founded in 2007 by long-time independent editor/publishers and partners Diane Kistner and Robert S. King, the press incorporated as a nonprofit in 2012. A number of our editors are distinguished poets and authors in their own right, and we have been actively involved in the small press movement going back to the early seventies.

The FutureCycle Poetry Book Prize and honorarium is awarded annually for the best full-length volume of poetry we publish in a calendar year. We are dedicated to giving all authors we publish the care their work deserves, making our catalog of titles the most distinguished it can be, and paying forward any earnings to fund more great books.

We've learned a few things about independent publishing over the years. We've also evolved a unique, resilient publishing model that allows us to focus mainly on vetting and preserving for posterity the most books of exceptional quality without becoming overwhelmed with bookkeeping and mailing, fundraising activities, or taxing editorial and production "bubbles." To find out more about what we are doing, come see us at www.futurecycle.org.

www.ingramcontent.com/pod-product-compliance
Lightning Source LLC
LaVergne TN
LVHW051806080426
835511LV00019B/3417